DOG BREEDS

GERMAN SHORTHAIRED POINTERS

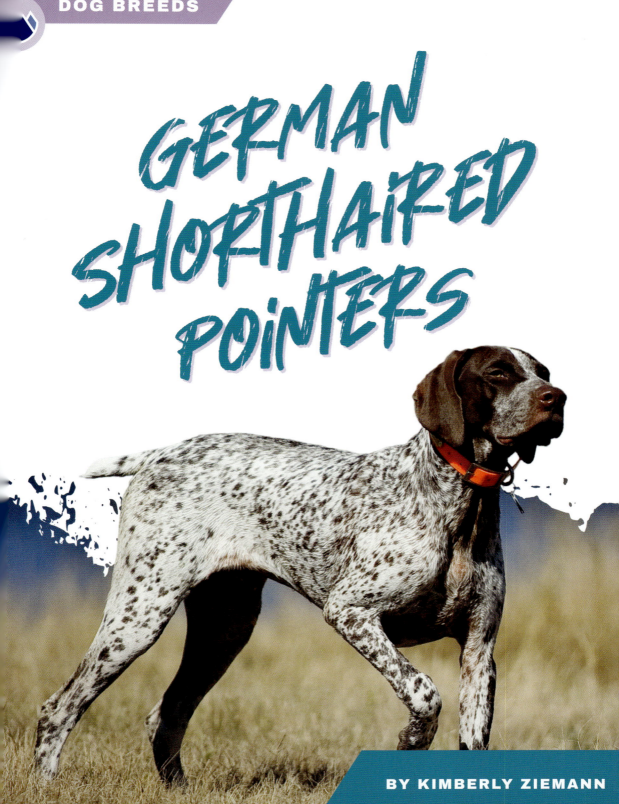

BY KIMBERLY ZIEMANN

WWW.APEXEDITIONS.COM

Copyright © 2025 by Apex Editions, Mendota Heights, MN 55120. All rights reserved. No part of this book may be reproduced or utilized in any form or by any means without written permission from the publisher.

Apex is distributed by North Star Editions:
sales@northstareditions.com | 888-417-0195

Produced for Apex by Red Line Editorial.

Photographs ©: Shutterstock Images, cover, 1, 6, 7, 8–9, 12, 13, 14, 16–17, 19, 21, 25, 26–27, 29; iStockphoto, 4–5, 10–11, 18, 22–23, 24

Library of Congress Control Number: 2023921769

ISBN
978-1-63738-909-6 (hardcover)
978-1-63738-949-2 (paperback)
979-8-89250-046-3 (ebook pdf)
979-8-89250-007-4 (hosted ebook)

Printed in the United States of America
Mankato, MN
082024

NOTE TO PARENTS AND EDUCATORS

Apex books are designed to build literacy skills in striving readers. Exciting, high-interest content attracts and holds readers' attention. The text is carefully leveled to allow students to achieve success quickly. Additional features, such as bolded glossary words for difficult terms, help build comprehension.

TABLE OF CONTENTS

CHAPTER 1
ON THE HUNT 4

CHAPTER 2
HUNTING DOGS 10

CHAPTER 3
APPEARANCE 16

CHAPTER 4
CARE AND TRAINING 22

COMPREHENSION QUESTIONS • 28
GLOSSARY • 30
TO LEARN MORE • 31
ABOUT THE AUTHOR • 31
INDEX • 32

CHAPTER 1

ON THE HUNT

Greta is a German shorthaired pointer. She and her owner are hunting for birds. Greta runs through the field and sniffs the air.

German shorthaired pointers have an excellent sense of smell.

When a dog points, it uses its nose to show which way a smell is.

Greta smells a pheasant. She slowly moves forward and lifts one paw. She lowers her head to point her nose toward the bird. Then she holds very still.

BIRD DOG

German shorthaired pointers help people hunt many types of birds. They track land birds such as pheasants and quail. They also hunt water birds such as ducks and geese.

Pheasants often live in grassy fields.

Greta's owner spots the bird. The pheasant flies up out of the grass. The owner shoots it. Greta runs to bring it back.

FAST FACT

German shorthaired pointers are also called GSPs.

Hunting dogs can help people find birds in tall grass.

CHAPTER 2

Hunting Dogs

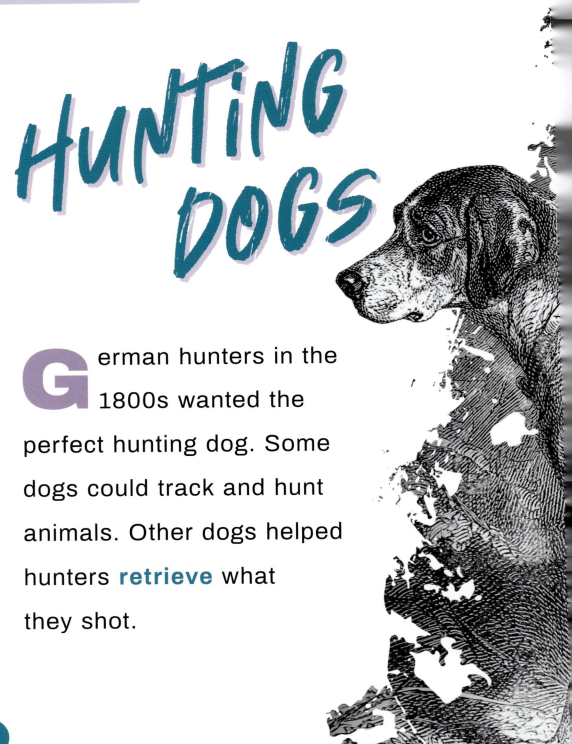

German hunters in the 1800s wanted the perfect hunting dog. Some dogs could track and hunt animals. Other dogs helped hunters **retrieve** what they shot.

Dogs have helped hunters find and catch animals for thousands of years.

People wanted one dog that could do all these things. So, they mixed several **breeds** together. Some breeds were pointers. Another was the bloodhound. By the late 1800s, the GSP breed was created.

Bloodhounds are known for their great sense of smell.

English pointers are fast sporting dogs. They were added to the GSP breed mix for their speed.

SPORTING DOGS

Dog breeds are split into different groups. German shorthaired pointers belong to the sporting group. Sporting dogs often hunt and retrieve. They are active and smart.

People brought GSPs to the United States in 1925. Today, the dogs are popular pets. Many owners still use them to hunt.

FAST FACT
Some GSPs work as police dogs.

◀ Some GSPs work as sniffer dogs. They are trained to find bombs and other explosives.

CHAPTER 3

APPEARANCE

German shorthaired pointers are medium-sized dogs. They stand about 23 inches (58 cm) tall. They can weigh 45 to 70 pounds (20 to 32 kg).

People bred GSPs to be big enough to hunt deer and other large animals.

Some GSPs have solid black fur. But most have several colors.

GSPs have short fur. Their fur can be **liver**, white, brown, or black. Many GSPs have small spots on their fur. This pattern is called ticking.

WATER DOGS

German shorthaired pointers were bred to hunt water birds. GSPs are great swimmers. Their short coat helps them move quickly in the water. It is also **water-resistant**.

Many GSPs love swimming, but they can get cold easily.

GSPs are slim but muscular. They have strong legs. They have wide heads and long, floppy ears. The dogs' tails are sometimes **docked**.

FAST FACT

GSPs' long ears can trap dirt. Owners should clean their dog's ears often.

German shorthaired pointers can run fast thanks to their long legs.

CHAPTER 4

CARE AND TRAINING

German shorthaired pointers are energetic. They should get one to two hours of exercise each day. Owners should have them run and play.

Many GSPs enjoy going on runs and hikes with their owners.

GSPs may dig holes if they get bored.

Training is also important. Owners should start when dogs are puppies. They should work with their dogs each day. GSPs may chew things if they are bored or left alone too long.

ACTIVE DOGS

GSPs learn quickly. Many compete in dog sports. For example, some GSPs do **agility** events. They learn to run quickly through **obstacle** courses.

Agility courses often include hurdles that dogs jump over.

German shorthaired pointers want to chase **prey**. Owners should keep dogs in fenced areas so they don't run off. And they should use leashes on walks.

FAST FACT

GSPs love playing with older children. But they might play too rough for younger kids.

A leash can help make sure a GSP won't run away and get lost.

COMPREHENSION QUESTIONS

Write your answers on a separate piece of paper.

1. Write a few sentences explaining the main ideas of Chapter 2.

2. Would you prefer to own a calm dog or an active dog? Why?

3. How much do German shorthaired pointers weigh?
   - A. less than 20 pounds (9 kg)
   - B. up to 45 pounds (20 kg)
   - C. up to 70 pounds (32 kg)

4. How would learning quickly help GSPs do dog sports?
   - A. Owners could teach GSPs many tricks.
   - B. Owners could teach GSPs only a few tricks.
   - C. GSPs would not need training.

5. What does **muscular** mean in this book?

GSPs are slim but muscular. They have strong legs.

    A. not very big or strong
    B. able to move with speed and power
    C. needing to move very slowly

6. What does **energetic** mean in this book?

German shorthaired pointers are energetic. They should get one to two hours of exercise each day.

    A. active
    B. hungry
    C. lazy

Answer key on page 32.

GLOSSARY

agility
A sport where dogs run through an obstacle course.

breeds
Specific types of dogs that have their own looks and abilities.

docked
Cut short or clipped off.

liver
A reddish-brown color.

obstacle
A thing that blocks the way.

prey
Animals that are hunted by other animals.

retrieve
To go get something and bring it back.

water-resistant
Not allowing water to pass through easily.

TO LEARN MORE

BOOKS

Norton, Elisabeth. *Sniffer Dogs*. Mendota Heights, MN: Apex Editions, 2023.

Oachs, Emily Rose. *Sporting Dogs*. Minneapolis: Bellwether Media, 2021.

Pearson, Marie. *Dogs*. Mankato, MN: The Child's World, 2020.

ONLINE RESOURCES

Visit **www.apexeditions.com** to find links and resources related to this title.

ABOUT THE AUTHOR

Kimberly Ziemann lives in Nebraska with her husband and three daughters. She works as a reading teacher with elementary students. While she enjoys writing books for children, her favorite activity is reading. She also loves playing with her two dogs and snuggling with her cat.

INDEX

A
agility, 25

B
birds, 4, 6–8, 19
bloodhounds, 12
breeds, 12–13

E
exercise, 22

F
fur, 18

H
hunting, 4, 7, 10, 13, 15, 19

P
pheasants, 6–8
police, 15
prey, 26

R
retrieving, 10, 13

T
ticking, 18
tracking, 7, 10
training, 24

U
United States, 15

W
water, 7, 19

ANSWER KEY:
1. Answers will vary; 2. Answers will vary; 3. C; 4. A; 5. B; 6. A